ORIGINAL KEYS for SINGERS

THE BEATLES

VOCAL • PIANO

T0071641

ISBN 978-1-4584-2307-8

HAL•LEONARD®
CORPORATION

7777 W. BLUEMOUND RD. P.O. BOX 13819 MILWAUKEE, WI 53213

Visit Hal Leonard Online at
www.halleonard.com

AND I LOVE HER

Words and Music by JOHN LENNON
and PAUL McCARTNEY

4

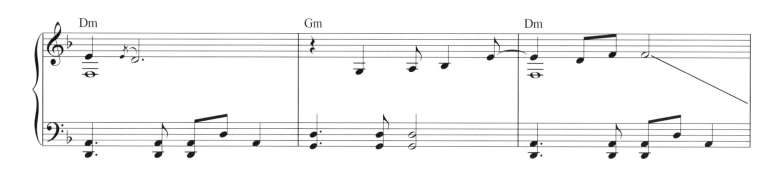

Bright are the stars ___ that shine; ___

dark is the sky. _____ I know this

Dm   B♭   C7

love of mine _   will nev - er die. _____   And I love _

F6   Gm

_ her. _____

F

Gm   D

BLACKBIRD

Words and Music by JOHN LENNON
and PAUL McCARTNEY

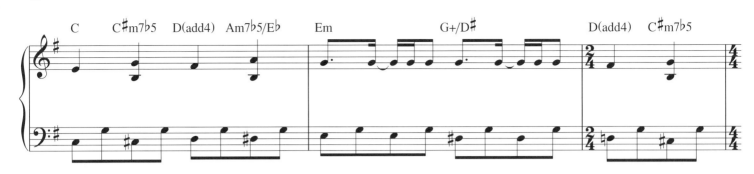

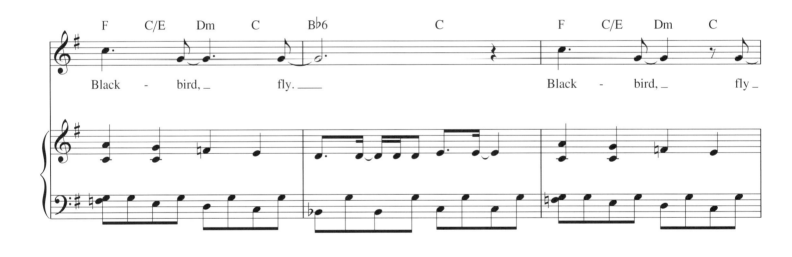

Black - bird, __ fly. ___ Black - bird, __ fly _

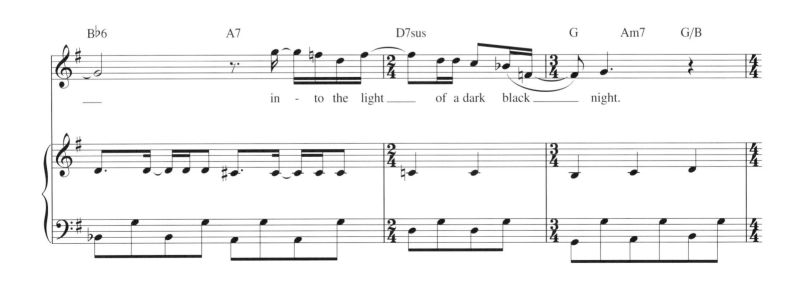

__ in - to the light ___ of a dark black ___ night.

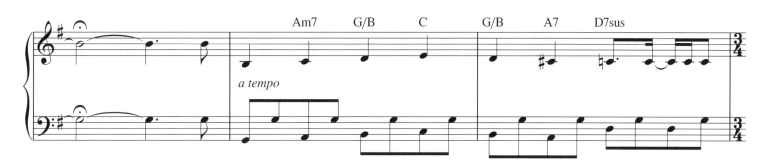

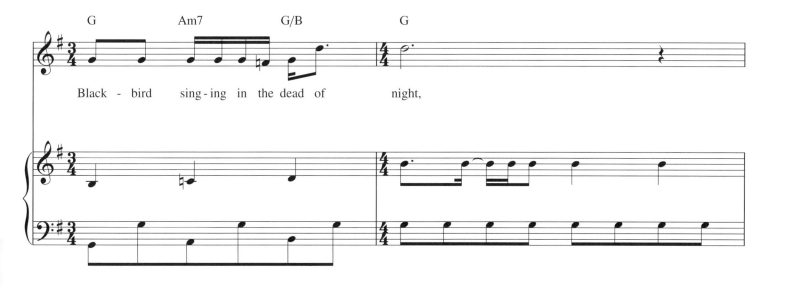

Black - bird sing - ing in the dead of night,

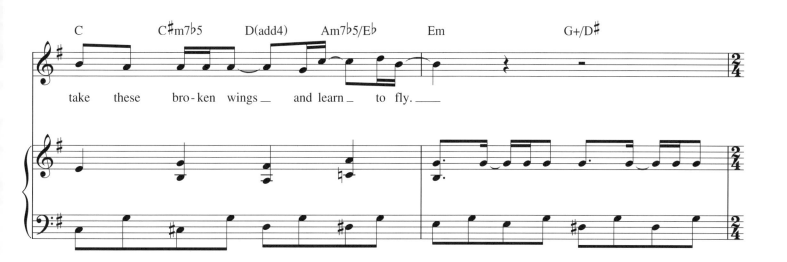

take these bro - ken wings ___ and learn ___ to fly. ___

CAN'T BUY ME LOVE

Words and Music by JOHN LENNON
and PAUL McCARTNEY

Guitar solo arranged for piano R.H.

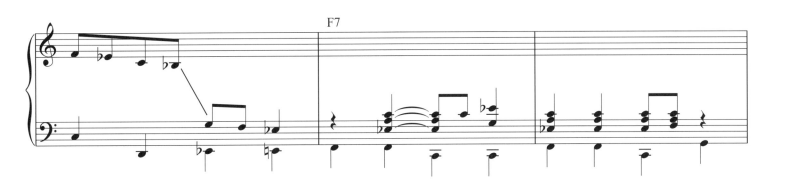

D.S. al Coda

Buy   me   love; ___

ELEANOR RIGBY

Words and Music by JOHN LENNON
and PAUL McCARTNEY

Moderately fast

Ah, _____ look at all _____ the lone - ly peo - ple.

Ah, _____ look at all _____ the lone - ly peo -

- ple.   El - ea - nor Rig - by

THE FOOL ON THE HILL

Words and Music by JOHN LENNON
and PAUL McCARTNEY

Slowly, with feeling

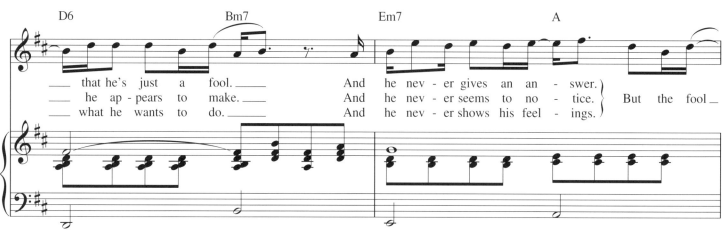

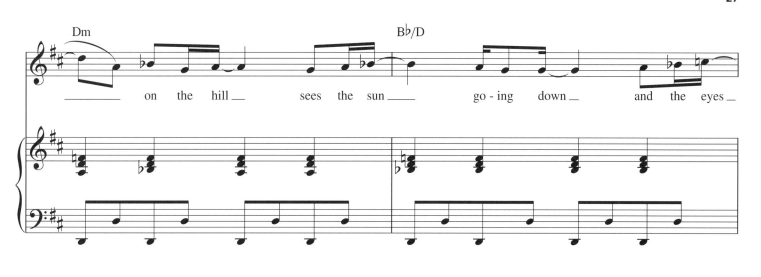

on the hill ___ sees the sun ___ go-ing down ___ and the eyes ___

in his head ___ see the world ___ spin-ning 'round. ___

But

GOOD NIGHT

Words and Music by JOHN LENNON
and PAUL McCARTNEY

Moderately slow, in 2

Pedal ad lib. throughout

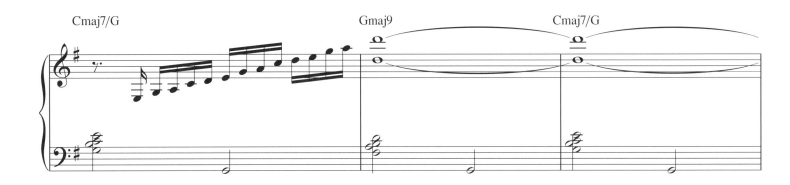

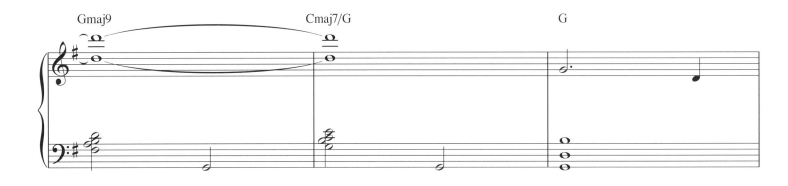

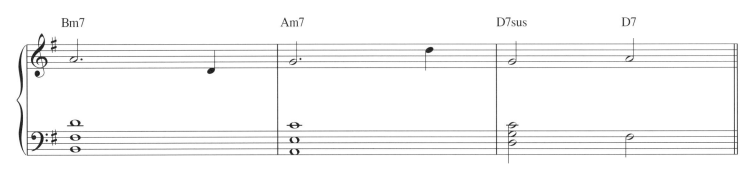

GOT TO GET YOU INTO MY LIFE

Words and Music by JOHN LENNON
and PAUL McCARTNEY

HERE COMES THE SUN

Words and Music by
GEORGE HARRISON

dut - n - du - du. Here comes the sun, ___ and I ___ say

it's all ___ right.

HERE, THERE AND EVERYWHERE

Words and Music by JOHN LENNON
and PAUL McCARTNEY

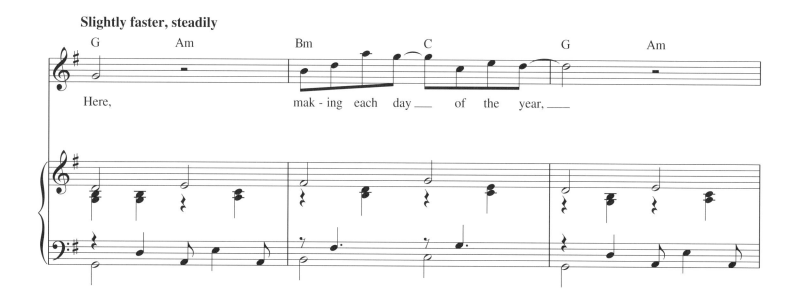

HEY JUDE

Words and Music by JOHN LENNON
and PAUL McCARTNEY

Moderately slow

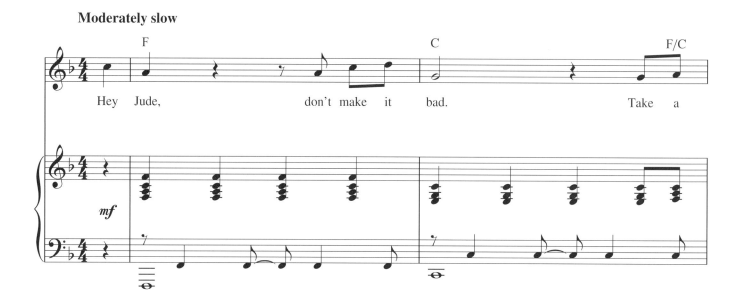

Hey   Jude,   don't make it bad.   Take a

sad   song ____ and make it   bet - ter. ____   Re - mem-ber   to let her in - to your

heart.   Then you can start ____   to make it ____ bet - ter.   Hey

na, na, na, na, hey Jude.)

(Na, na, na, na, na, na, na,

na, na, na, na, hey Jude.)

(Na, na, na, na, na, na, na,

na, na, na, na, hey __ Jude.) __

(Na, na, na, na, na, na, na,

Repeat and Fade

na, na, na, na, hey __ Jude.) __

Optional Ending

na, na, na, na, hey __ Jude.) __

molto rit.

I WILL

Words and Music by JOHN LENNON
and PAUL McCARTNEY

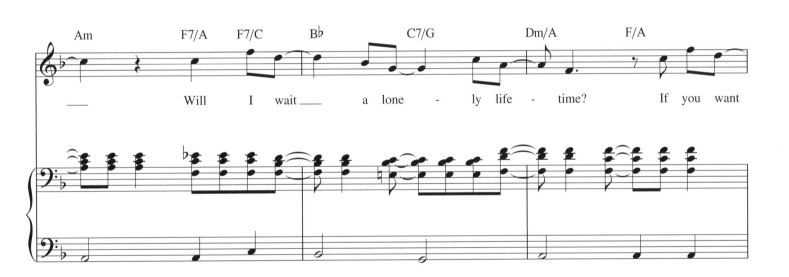

LADY MADONNA

Words and Music by JOHN LENNON
and PAUL McCARTNEY

LET IT BE

Words and Music by JOHN LENNON
and PAUL McCARTNEY

To Coda

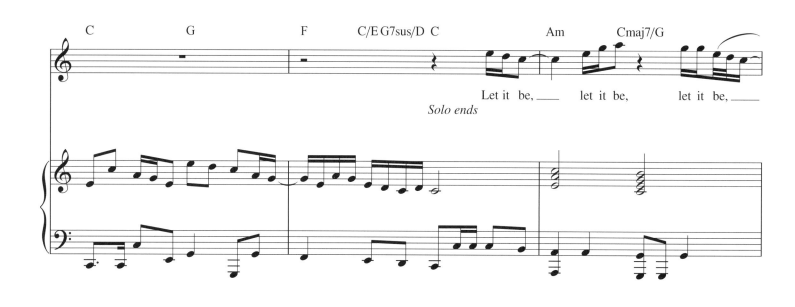

Let it be, ___ let it be, ___ let it be, ___

Solo ends

___ let it be. ___ Whis - per words ___ of wis - dom: "Let it be." ___

THE LONG AND WINDING ROAD

Words and Music by JOHN LENNON
and PAUL McCARTNEY

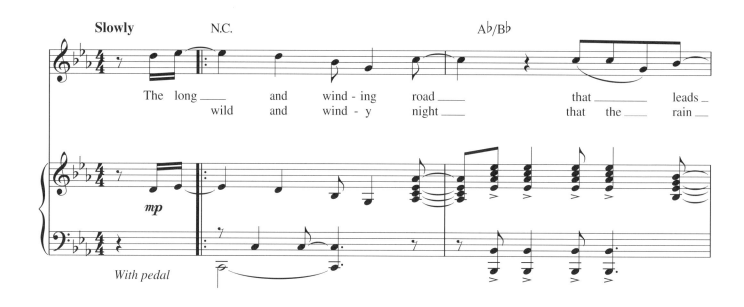

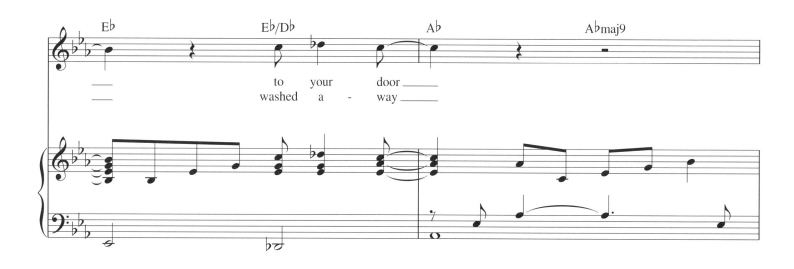

LUCY IN THE SKY WITH DIAMONDS

Words and Music by JOHN LENNON
and PAUL McCARTNEY

Moderately slow

N.C.

mp

With pedal

Pic - ture your - self in a boat on a riv - er, with
bridge by a foun - tain, with where
train in a sta - tion, with

tan - ge - rine _____ trees and mar - ma - lade _____
rock - ing horse _____ peo - ple eat marsh - mal - low _____
plas - ti - cene _____ por - ters with look - ing glass _____

F   F/C   F/D   N.C.

skies.   Some - bod - y _____ calls _____ you, you
pies.   Ev - 'ry - one _____ smiles _____ as you
ties.   Sud - den - ly, _____ some - one is

MICHELLE

Words and Music by JOHN LENNON
and PAUL McCARTNEY

say the on - ly words ___ I know that you'll un - der -

stand, my Mi - chelle. *(vocal 1st time only)*
Instrumental solo

Repeat and Fade

Optional Ending

NORWEGIAN WOOD
(This Bird Has Flown)

Words and Music by JOHN LENNON
and PAUL McCARTNEY

Moderately fast

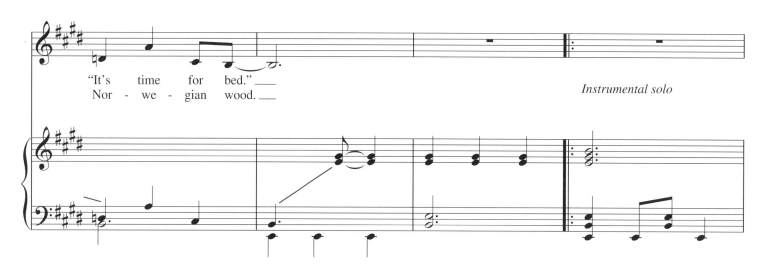

"It's time for bed." ___
Nor - we - gian wood. ___

Instrumental solo

To Coda ⊕

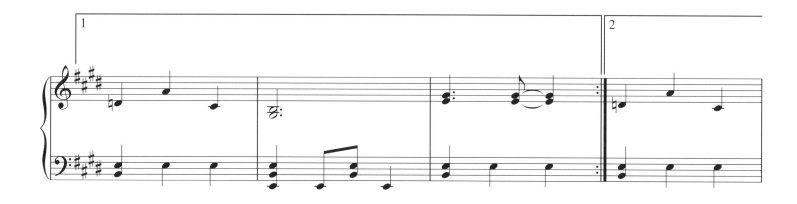

1

2

D.S. al Coda

She

CODA ⊕

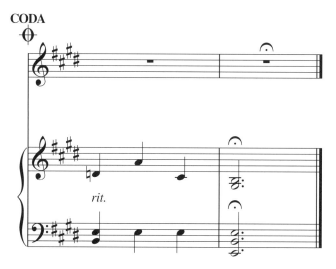

rit.

OB-LA-DI, OB-LA-DA

Words and Music by JOHN LENNON
and PAUL McCARTNEY

Moderately

With pedal

Des-mond has a bar-row in the mar-ket - place; ___ Mol-
Des-mond takes a trol-ley to the jewel-er's store, ___ buys ___

- ly is the sing-er in a band.
___ a twen-ty car-at gold-en ring; ___ (Ring!) ___ Des-
Des-takes ___

- mond says to Mol-ly, "Girl, I like your face;" ___ and Mol-ly
___ it back to Mol-ly wait-ing at the door, ___ and as he

In a cou - ple of years, they have built a home sweet home,

with a cou - ple of kids run - ning in the yard of

Des - mond and Mol - ly Jones.

PENNY LANE

Words and Music by JOHN LENNON
and PAUL McCARTNEY

In Pen - ny Lane, ___ there is a bar - ber show - ing
shel - ter in the mid - dle of a

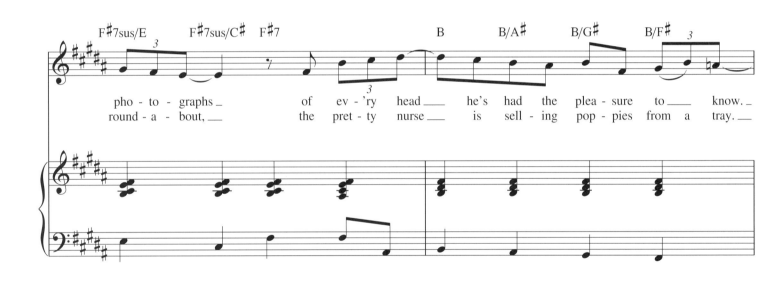

pho - to - graphs ___ of ev - 'ry head ___ he's had the plea - sure to ___ know. ___
round - a - bout, ___ the pret - ty nurse ___ is sell - ing pop - pies from a tray. ___

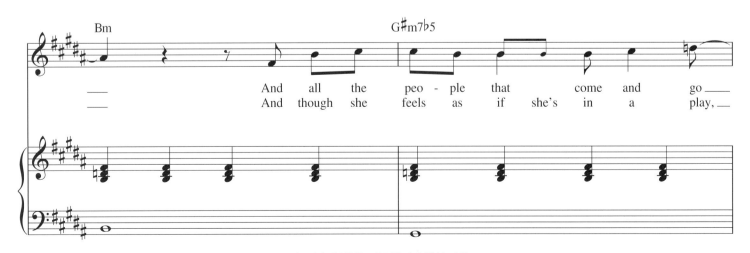

And all the peo - ple that come and go ___
And though she feels as if she's in a play, ___

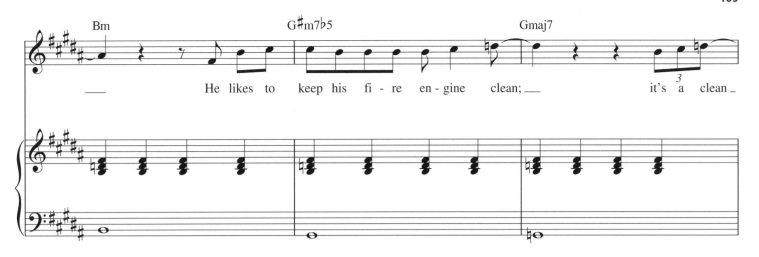

He likes to keep his fi - re en - gine clean; it's a clean

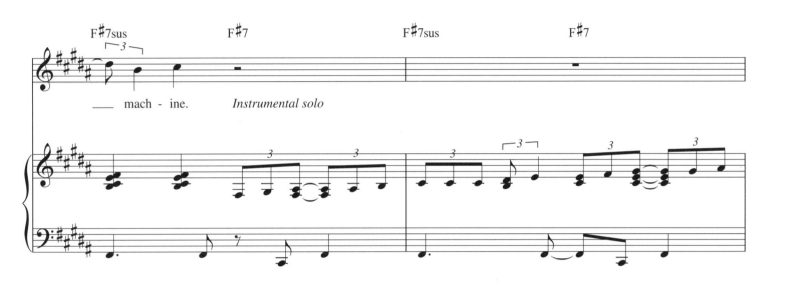

mach - ine. *Instrumental solo*

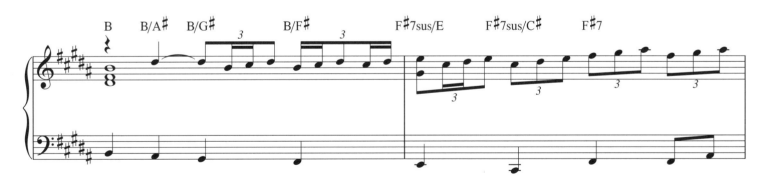

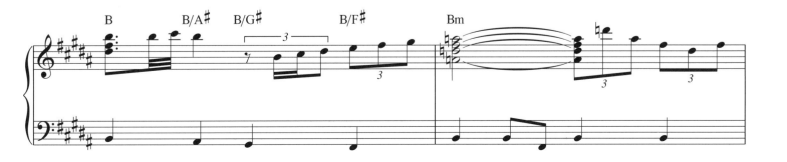

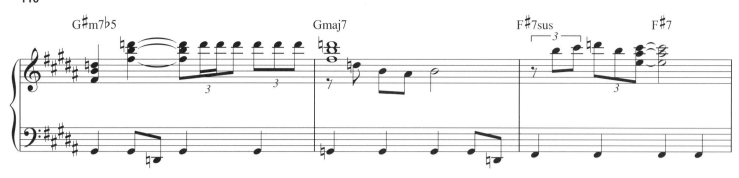

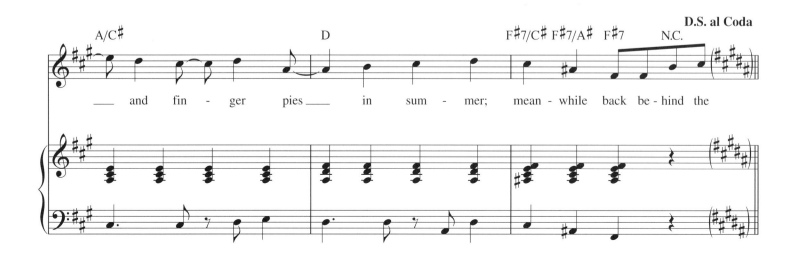

SOMETHING

Words and Music by
GEORGE HARRISON

Slowly, with feeling

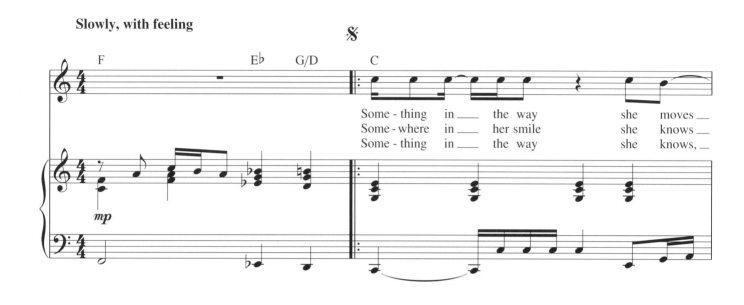

Something in ___ the way _____ she moves
Somewhere in ___ her smile _____ she knows
Something in ___ the way _____ she knows, _____

___ at - tracts ___ me like _____ no oth - er lov -
___ that I ___ don't need _____ no oth - er lov -
___ and all ___ I have to do is think ___

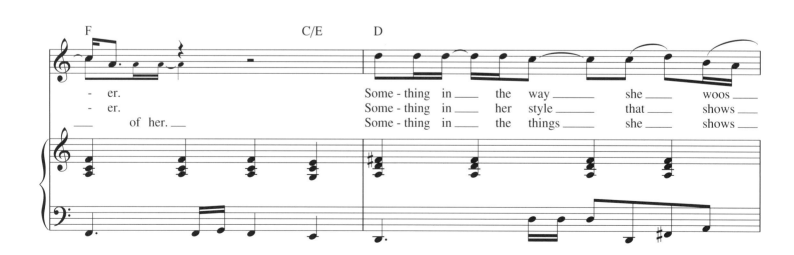

- er.
- er.
___ of her. ___

Some - thing in ___ the way _____ she _____ woos _____
Some - thing in ___ her style _____ that _____ shows _____
Some - thing in ___ the things _____ she _____ shows _____

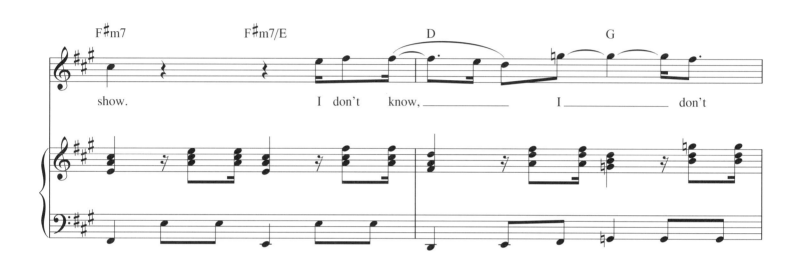

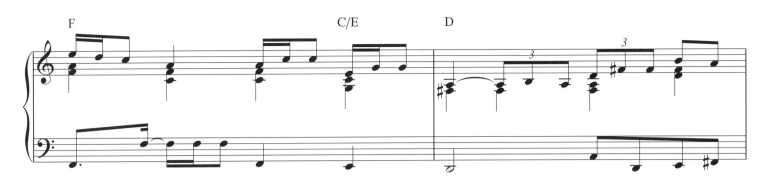

WHEN I'M SIXTY-FOUR

Words and Music by JOHN LENNON
and PAUL McCARTNEY

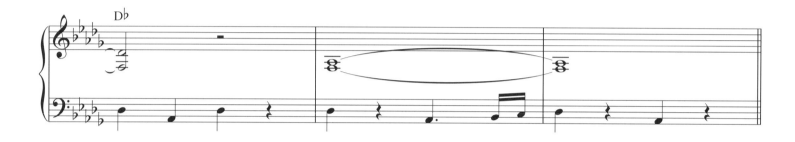

When I get old - er, los - ing my hair, ___ man - y years from now, ___
I could be hand - y mend - ing a fuse ___ when your lights have gone. ___
Send me a post - card, drop me a line, ___ stat - ing point of view. ___

will you still be send - ing me a
You can knit a sweat - er by the
In - di - cate pre - cise - ly what you

Gb / Ab / Db

I could stay with you.
Ve - ra, Chuck with and you. Dave.

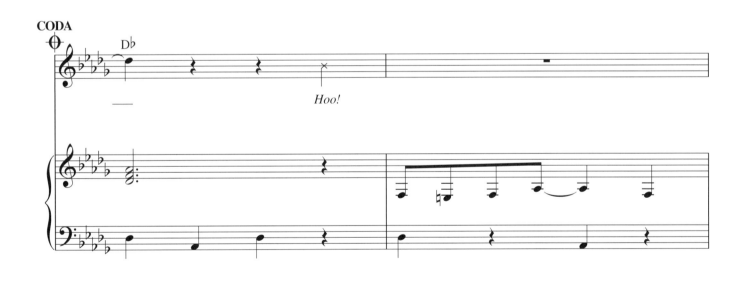

1 N.C.

2 N.C.

D.S. al Coda

CODA

Db

Hoo!

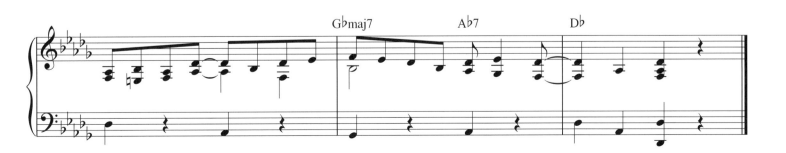

Gbmaj7 / Ab7 / Db

WHILE MY GUITAR GENTLY WEEPS

Words and Music by
GEORGE HARRISON

Half-time feel

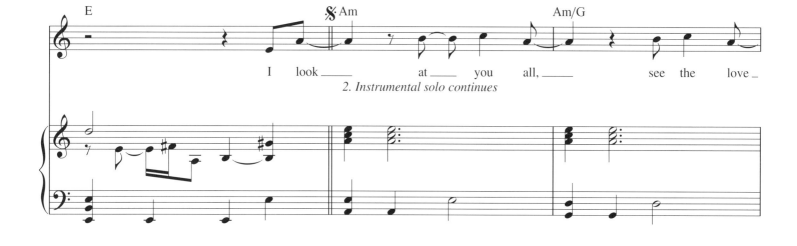

I look ___ at ___ you all, ___ see the love _
2. Instrumental solo continues

___ there ___ that's sleep - ing,   while ___ my ___ gui - tar

WITH A LITTLE HELP
FROM MY FRIENDS

Words and Music by JOHN LENNON
and PAUL McCARTNEY

Moderate Shuffle

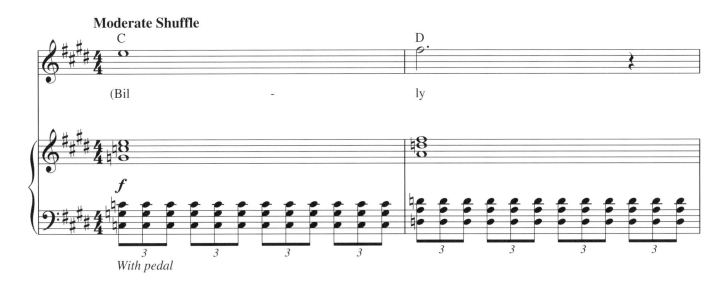

(Bil - ly

Shears!)

What would you think __ if I sang __
What do I do __ when my love __
(Would you be - lieve __ in a love __

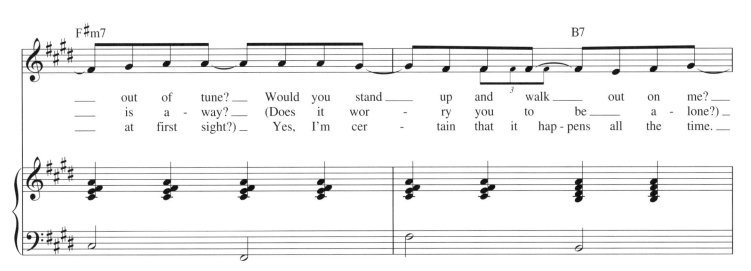

__ out of tune? __ Would you stand __ up and walk __ out on me? __
__ is a - way? __ (Does it wor - ry you to be __ a - lone?)
__ at first sight?) __ Yes, I'm cer - tain that it hap - pens all the time. __

YESTERDAY

Words and Music by
JOHN LENNON and PAUL McCARTNEY

YOU'VE GOT TO HIDE YOUR LOVE AWAY

Words and Music by JOHN LENNON
and PAUL McCARTNEY

Moderate Waltz

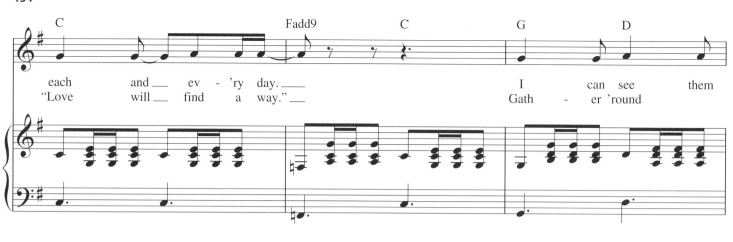

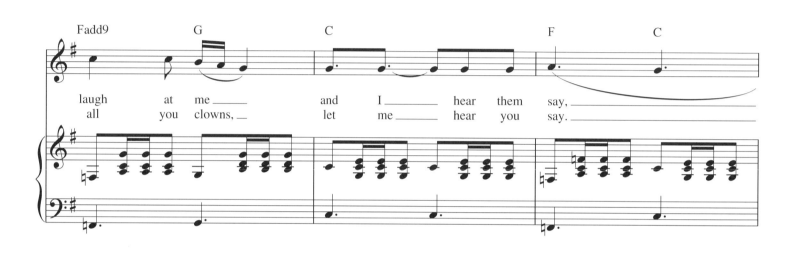

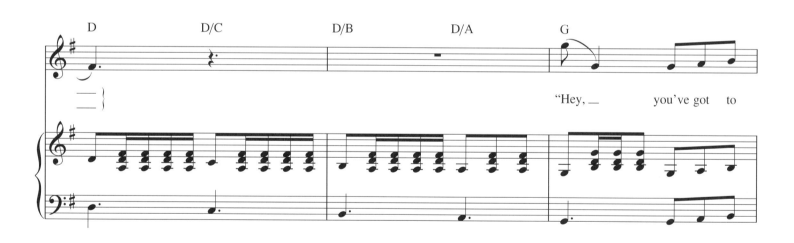

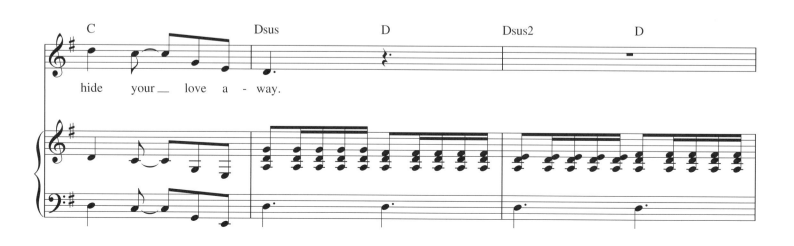

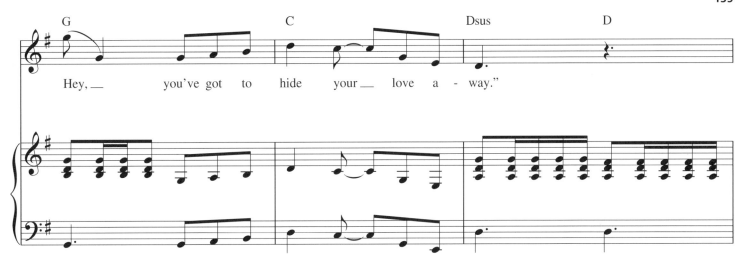

Hey, ___ you've got to hide your ___ love a - way."

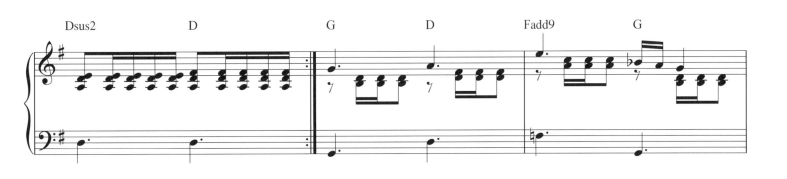

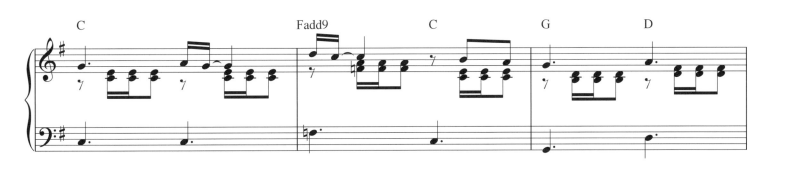